TIME

Caterina Rochat

Illustrated by
Alessandro Bartolozzi,
Giovanni Bernardi,
Sergio

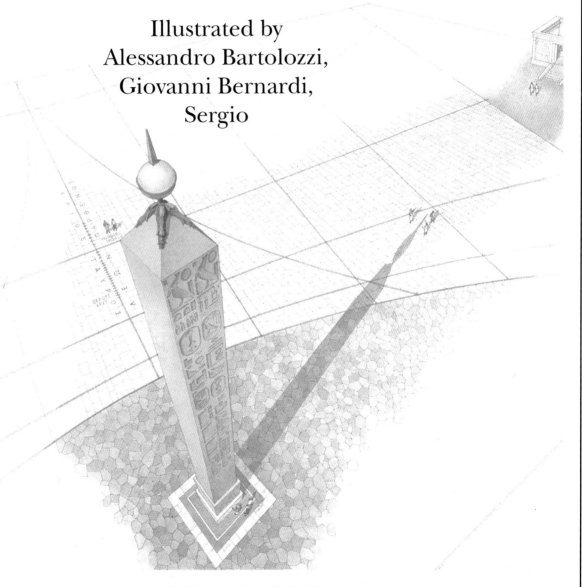

WATTS BOOKS

LONDON   NEW YORK   SYDNEY

DoGi

A Donati Giudici
Associati, Florence,
production.
Original title *Le
misure del tempo*
Text:
Caterina Rochat
Illustrations:
Alessandro
Bartolozzi,
Giovanni Bernardi,
Sergio
Designers:
Roberto Lari
Sabina Carandini

© 1995 By Donati
Guidici Associati srl
Florence,
Italy

First English edition
© 1995 Watts Books

Watts Books
96 Leonard Street
London
EC2A 4RH

Franklin Watts
Australia
14 Mars Cove
NSW 2066

UK ISBN
0 7496 1979 1

10 9 8 7 6 5 4 3 2 1

A CIP catalogue
record for this book
is available from the
British Library.

English translation by
Patricia Borlenghi

Edited by
Janet De Saulles

HOW TO USE THIS BOOK

SUBJECT
The introductory
paragraphs present
the main ideas of
each chapter.

EXPLANATION
The main subject
of each chapter is
brought to life with
beautiful large
illustrations. Short
captions draw
attention to
interesting details.

GLOSSARY
Technical or more
difficult words are
explained in the
glossary, found at
the back of the
book.

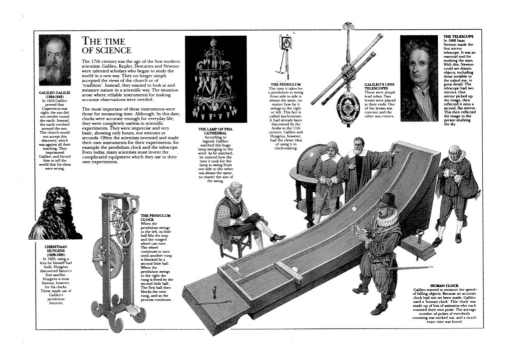

**HISTORICAL
BACKGROUND**
The historical
background of
each area is given,
and later
developments are
explored.

LEADING FIGURES
People who have
contributed to the
development of
different
inventions or
theories are
included.

EXPERIMENTS
Easy and enjoyable
experiments are
suggested, letting
the readers
discover for
themselves some of
the scientific
principles looked
at in this book.

CREDITS

The illustrations in this book, original and
previously unpublished, have been produced
under the direction of DoGi, who holds
copyright.
ILLUSTRATIONS: Alessandro Bartolozzi (4a, 4c,
4d, 6b, 7g, 7h, 8-9, 11b, 11c, 12a, 16a, 21a,
21b, 22b, 23c, 23b, 24b, 26b, 32b, 32c, 33a,
34a, 34b, 42-43); Giovanni Bernardi (5a, 6-7,
10-11, 20-21, 22-23, 24b, 26b, 32b, 32c, 33a,
34a, 34b, 42-43); Giacinto Gaudenzi (5b,
26a); Roberto Lari (17e, 17b, 17c, 17d);
Sandro Rabatti (12-13); Claudia Saraceni
(7d, 7e, 7f, 19b, 33b); Sergio (4b, 14-15, 18a,
19c, 21c, 24-25, 28-29, 30-31, 32a, 35-36a,
36b, 37a, 38-39, 40-41, 44-45); Thomas
Troyer (7a, 7b, 7c, 12b, 22e).
COVER: Giovanni Bernardi
FRONTISPIECE: Giovanni Bernardi

PHOTOGRAPHS: ACE (5b); Archivio Cinema
Nuovo (37c); Archivio Citizen (43a);
Archivio CONI (40A, 40B, 41B, 41C); (Archivio
DoGi (10, 18b, 22, 24d, 28a); Archivio
Franco Cosimo Panini (30b); Archivio NASA
(9, 43b); British Transport Museum,
London(35B); Carlo Cantini, Florence (20a,
28b, 39c, 41a); Henry Ford Museum,
Dearborn, Michigan (37a); Musée National
de l'Horlogerie, La Chaux des Fonds (5b,
35a, 38b, 39b); Musée National des
Techniques, Paris 33a); Museo Egizio, Turin
(13a, 45b); Museo Nazionale della Scienza e
della Tecnica, Milan (26); Museo di Storia
della Scienza, Florence (24a, 24b, 31, 32);
Roger-Viollet, Paris (20b); Science Museum,
London (13b); Sequoia National Park, USA
(45a); Uhrenmuseum, Wuppertal
(38a).Vatican Museum (4b);
The publishers would like to thank the

following institutions for giving permission
to reproduce the works: Anon., *Julius Caesar*,
Rome, Musei Vaticani, Ist century (4b, 16a);
Anon., *Isacco Newton*, Bologna, Biblioteca
Universitaria, 18th century. (31b); P. Bruegel,
Battle between Carnival and Lent,
Künsthistorisches Museum, Vienna, 1599
(16c); L. Carracci, *Portrait of Gregory XIII*,
detail (4a, 16b); S. del Piombo, *Christopher
Colombus*, New York, Metropolitan Museum
(33b); Paleolithic bone engravings from Les
Eyzies, Dordogne (18a); Pelizza da Volpedo,
The Fourth State, Milan, Galleria di Brera,
1908 (37b); J. Sustermans, *Galileo Galilei*,
Florence, Uffizi, 17th century (30a).
DoGi has made every effort to contact all the
relevant copyright holders and apologise for
any omissions or errors that may have been
made. Any corrections will be made in the
next editions of this work.

CONTENTS

WHAT YOU WILL LEARN FROM THIS BOOK

There are many ways of measuring time. The oldest of these only made note of the change of the seasons, and the passing of months and days. Such measurements were based on the position of the sun and the changing face of the moon. They were also based on the times when animals migrated and when plants flowered.

More recent forms of measuring time start to divide time into smaller and smaller divisions of hours, minutes, seconds – even hundredths and thousandths of seconds. The reason behind changes in ways of measuring is that every type of society looks at time in terms of its own pace of life and activities. In the hunters' or farmers' society the pace is slow. In societies such as ours, which are based on industry, technology and communications, the pace is very quick, with times worked out to the nearest second or split second.

NATURE'S TIME
The sun, with the alternation of day and night, has always been the basic measure of time. At nightfall, there is a drop in temperature which forces life itself to slow down: the lack of light interrupts the growth of plants and slows down the activities of many animals.

THE UNDERSTANDING OF TIME
Our knowledge of time comes from observing natural events over thousands upon thousands of years. Our ancestors realised that certain events repeated themselves again and again in a precise pattern. The sun rose and set, leaves sprouted and later fell from trees, living beings were born and then died. Children, as well as adults, understood time in the same way, learning to distinguish between the idea of 'before' and 'after'.

THE DAY AS A UNIT OF TIME
By observing the order of natural events, people learned to foretell the future of certain things. They saw that when one event happened, a second one would follow. What people next learned, was to measure the gap between the two events. The gap between the dawn of one day and the next – ie the length of a day – was one of the first units of measuring.

CALENDARS
The calendar was invented to help calculate and forecast events. The first calendars were a list of the main natural events in the order in which they occured. These included the changes of the moon, the appearance and disappearance of stars, the flowering of plants, and the migration of animals. The calendars indicated the interval of time between one event and the next. The calendar used in the West is called Gregorian, after Pope Gregory XIII who produced it in 1582.

A TIME FOR EVERY ACTIVITY
The method of measuring time was determined by different activities. Farmers measured time by the seasons, since these were essential for their work in the fields; shepherds took note of the lunar months because these helped them to keep track of breeding periods; artisans used days as a unit for measuring work. Finally, ancient priests used the stars to interpret the divine order of things.

CHRONICLES
While calendars were used for forecasting, chronicles were used as reminders. The passing of time was counted in years and recorded from dates considered essential for each particular society. For example, the Romans took their starting date as the mythical founding of Rome, and counted the years from 753 BC.

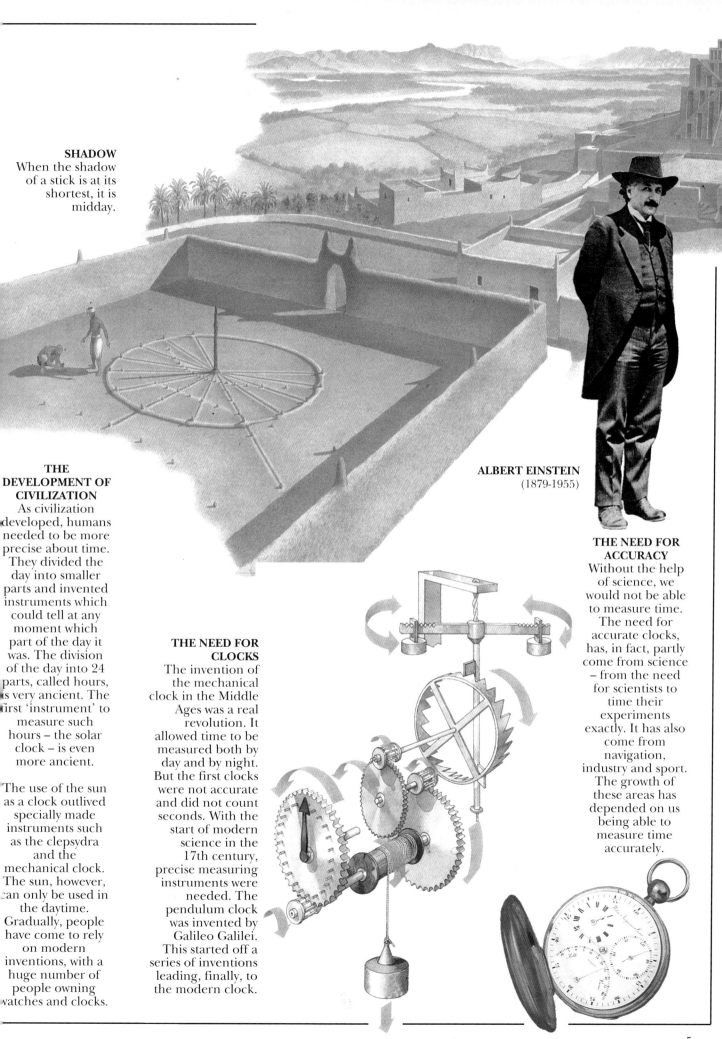

SHADOW
When the shadow of a stick is at its shortest, it is midday.

ALBERT EINSTEIN
(1879-1955)

THE DEVELOPMENT OF CIVILIZATION

As civilization developed, humans needed to be more precise about time. They divided the day into smaller parts and invented instruments which could tell at any moment which part of the day it was. The division of the day into 24 parts, called hours, is very ancient. The first 'instrument' to measure such hours – the solar clock – is even more ancient.

The use of the sun as a clock outlived specially made instruments such as the clepsydra and the mechanical clock. The sun, however, can only be used in the daytime. Gradually, people have come to rely on modern inventions, with a huge number of people owning watches and clocks.

THE NEED FOR CLOCKS

The invention of the mechanical clock in the Middle Ages was a real revolution. It allowed time to be measured both by day and by night. But the first clocks were not accurate and did not count seconds. With the start of modern science in the 17th century, precise measuring instruments were needed. The pendulum clock was invented by Galileo Galilei. This started off a series of inventions leading, finally, to the modern clock.

THE NEED FOR ACCURACY

Without the help of science, we would not be able to measure time. The need for accurate clocks, has, in fact, partly come from science – from the need for scientists to time their experiments exactly. It has also come from navigation, industry and sport. The growth of these areas has depended on us being able to measure time accurately.

THE SUN AND SEASONS

As we look at the sun in the sky, its position appears to vary according to the time of day and to the seasons. It seems to form a curve in the sky as it rises in the east and sets in the west. It reaches its highest point at midday then, as it sets, it disappears behind the horizon. We now know that the sun only looks as if it is moving. In fact, it is the earth itself which is spinning, but around its own axis. This makes it seem as if the sun is moving.

However, our ancestors made many useful discoveries, simply by studying the sun's different positions. They noticed that the sun rises and sets at slightly different points during the year. They saw that the sun's height at midday is not always the same, and that the length of night and day changes at different times of the year. They also noticed that these variations go hand in hand with regular changes in nature. Such changes include the flowering of some plants, the migration of birds and the alternation of hot and cold periods. People came to see that time was made up of repeated seasonal cycles.

A BABYLONIAN FARMER
Assur is a Babylonian farmer. At dawn he checks the stones on the courtyard walls to find out the point at which the sun rises. Today it rose near the last stone on the right and the day will be short. But gradually the sun will rise more and more to the left. The days will lengthen and the weather will get warmer.

THE EARTH'S PASSAGE AROUND THE SUN
It takes the earth about 365 days (365.24) to rotate around the sun. We call this period a year. It spins with its axis tilted at about 23.25 degrees. It is this tilt which causes the seasons. In one year the two hemispheres are alternately tilted towards the sun or away from it.

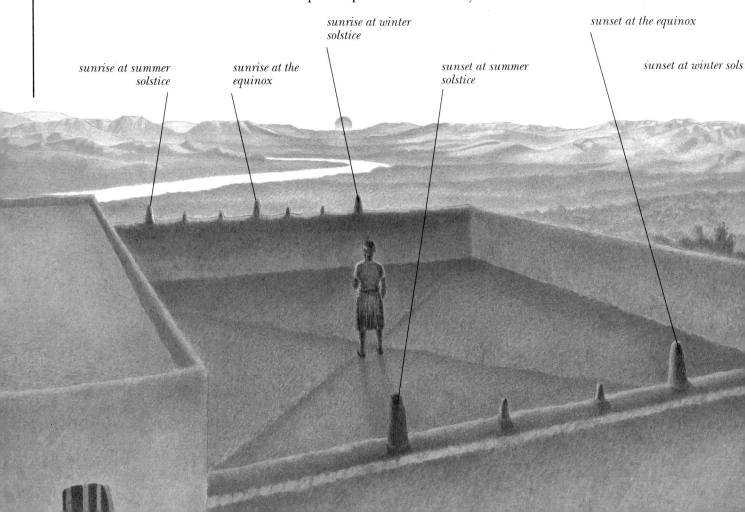

sunrise at winter solstice

sunset at the equinox

sunrise at summer solstice

sunrise at the equinox

sunset at summer solstice

sunset at winter sols

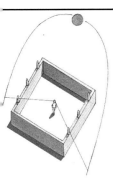

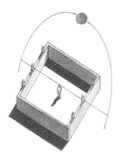

SUMMER
The sun rises in the north-east and sets in the north-west. Day is longer than night. At midday the sun is high and very hot.

SPRING AND AUTUMN
The sun rises in the east and sets in the west. Day and night are the same length. The midday sun is lower than in the summer.

WINTER
The sun rises in the south-east and sets in the south-west. Day is shorter than night and the midday sun is at its lowest point in the year. It is cold.

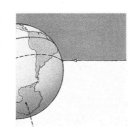

SUMMER SOLSTICE
This is usually 21 June, but it can be 20 or 22 June. It is the longest day of the year in the northern hemisphere. This day has the maximum amount of light.

EQUINOXES
These occur twice a year around 21 March and 22 September. The length of the day is equal to that of the night: 12 hours. This is true all over the world.

WINTER SOLSTICE
This is on 21 or 22 December and is the shortest day of the year in the northern hemisphere. The amount of light received is low.

A DAY
A day is the time it takes for the earth to rotate once around its own axis. The division of the day into 24 hours was adopted by Babylonian mathematicians. They counted with a number system based on 12 units rather than 10 units.

ZIGGURAT
This was the name given to the enormous brick pyramids from which Babylonian priests observed the moon and stars. They tried to predict events which happened on the earth, such as floods, wars and famines. From their work, the sciences of astrology and astronomy were born.

MESOPOTAMIA
Lying between the Tigris and Euphrates rivers, this country was the birthplace of an amazing Babylonian culture which began 4,000 years ago.

THE MOON AND MONTHS

By observing the sun, our ancestors divided time into seasons. By looking at the shape of the moon, they divided time into even smaller periods. They noticed that the changing shape of the moon always follows the same pattern. On some nights it is a full, shining disc. Then, as the nights go on, it slowly gets smaller and finally disappears. It remains hidden for a while and then reappears, shaped like a crescent. This grows daily, until it becomes a disc again.

People of ancient times noticed these changes were regular, and they used them to measure time in months and weeks. Between two full moons there are 29.5 days – one month. Each lunar phase lasts about seven days – one week. Today we know that the moon does not really change shape. It is actually a solid sphere which travels around the earth. It is its position in relation to the sun which changes, making it appear different shapes to us.

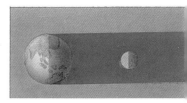

THE ECLIPSE OF THE MOON
About once a year, the earth's shadow falls over the moon, hiding it from our sight for a short time. This is called an eclipse.

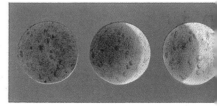

THE PHASES OF THE MOON

THE MOON'S PASSAGE AROUND EARTH
Just as the earth revolves round the sun, so the moon revolves round the earth. It takes about one month – 29.5 days – to do this. The moon's diameter is about 384,000 km – a quarter of the size of the earth's.

WAXING OR WANING?
To know if the moon is waxing (growing bigger) or waning (getting smaller), you just need to look at the crescent's shape. If the curve goes the same way as that of a capital D, it is waxing, but if it looks like a capital C, it is waning.

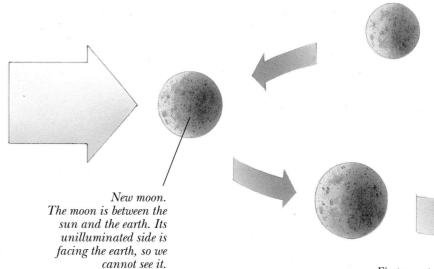

New moon. The moon is between the sun and the earth. Its unilluminated side is facing the earth, so we cannot see it.

First quarter. The moon forms an angle of 90° with the sun. We can see a half shape of the moon.

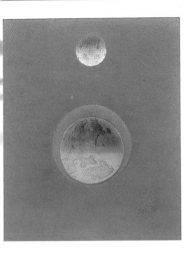

THE MOON'S INFLUENCE

The moon's movement has various effects on the earth. The most important is on the tides: the force of gravity from the moon raises the sea waters. The phases of the moon also influence plant and animal life.

It is important for farmers to observe the movement of the moon. Today, almanacs can be consulted. They are like calendars, advising which work should be done at what time.

LANDING ON THE MOON

The first contact with the moon was made in 1959 by a Soviet space probe, 'Luna II'. The first human to set foot on the moon, however, was the American astronaut, Neil Armstrong, in the famous mission of 21 July 1969. Since then US astronauts have returned another six times.

Last quarter. The moon forms an angle of 270° with the sun. From the earth, we can see half of the moon.

Full moon. Viewed from the earth, the sun and moon lie in two opposite directions, and the moon is completely lit up.

GREAT OBSERVATORIES

STONEHENGE
People started working on Sonehenge about 4,000 years ago. It was finished around 1400 BC. Hundreds of years of hard work were needed to position the stones to line up with the stars. Moving the boulders was an enormous job. The inside circle, built from bluestone which is only found 320 km away, must have been a tremendous task.

In ancient civilizations the sky was observed in order to measure time. It was also observed to understand the movement of the stars. These came to be seen as gods: people worshipped them, hoping for protection and advice. In this way, the first observatories were holy places, where ceremonies and religious rites were celebrated, and where the heavens were studied for clues about what would happen in the future.

Among such places, Stonehenge in England is among the most famous and fascinating. It was used as an observatory, with the stone altar a perfect point to observe movements in the above sky. Its other use was as a calendar: the positions of the stones helped to indicate important moments in the passage of the sun and moon. The priests could foresee not only the phases of the moon and sun, but could also predict eclipses.

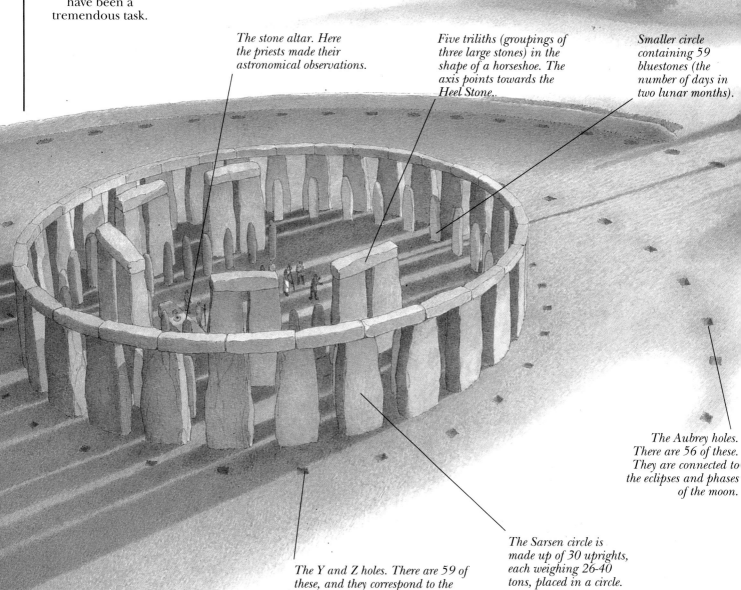

The stone altar. Here the priests made their astronomical observations.

Five triliths (groupings of three large stones) in the shape of a horseshoe. The axis points towards the Heel Stone..

Smaller circle containing 59 bluestones (the number of days in two lunar months).

The Aubrey holes. There are 56 of these. They are connected to the eclipses and phases of the moon.

The Y and Z holes. There are 59 of these, and they correspond to the number of days in two lunar months.

The Sarsen circle is made up of 30 uprights, each weighing 26-40 tons, placed in a circle.

The Avenue. This points in the direction of the sun at the summer solstice.

The Heel Stone. This was used to observe the sunrise. The surrounding hammered-in poles might have served to aim the moon into the centre of the monument.

THE MYSTERY OF STONEHENGE

Stonehenge's huge size, together with the strange arrangement of its stones, have given rise to many legends. According to one of the oldest, Stonehenge was built by Merlin, the famous wizard in King Arthur's court. Others say it is a 4,000 year-old extra-terrestial landing base!

SOLAR ECLIPSES

About once a year, the moon passes in front of the sun and hides it for a few minutes. This event can only be seen in places lining up with the sun and the moon at that moment. In ancient times people thought that this unexpected night was the result of the gods being angry. They attached huge importance to the forecast of eclipses.

THE EGYPTIAN CALENDAR

Life for ancient Egyptians depended on the Nile. When the river flooded, lime was carried to the fields, making them fertile. The ancient Egyptians realised that these floodings occurred regularly. In summer, with the appearance in the sky of the star Sirius, the river began to swell and flooded the valley. Then, once it had reached its highest level, the water slowly started to drop. A period of semi-drought would follow, at the end of which the waters of the Nile would start to rise again.

The Egyptians devised a calendar based on this cycle. The year began with one flooding – around July 19 in our calendar – and finished with the following flooding. The Egyptians divided the year into 12 months of 30 days, (adding 3 days at the end) and three seasons, each with 4 months. These seasons controlled their farming and daily life: Akhet was the flooding period, Peret the period where the waters began to drop and Shemu was the drought period.

18TH DYNASTY CALENDAR
The circles in the above calendar represent the 12 months of the year. Each circle has spaces reserved for the names of the 24 gods, one god standing for each hour of the day.

THE NILE VALLEY
Up to 90% of Egypt is desert. The ancient Egyptians made use of the fertile banks of the Nile, living on them and cultivating them for their food.

AKHET (FLOODING)
From around July 19 to mid-November, the Nile floods the cultivated lands. The farmers of ancient Egypt celebrated such flooding with feasts and holy ceremonies.

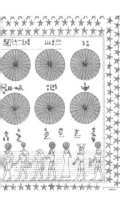

THREE CALENDARS

The Egyptians actually used three calendars. One was based on the Nile and was used for farming. The second was based on astronomical observations and set out the timing of ceremonies and magic festivals. These were held to celebrate the sun and the seasons and to secure their return. The third calendar was political. It counted off the years and days of each successive king of Egypt.

THE 'NILE METER'

The flooding of the Nile does not happen suddenly. Instead, starting from the south, the flooding slowly heads northwards. The ancient Egyptians invented the Nile meters to give an accurate forecast of when the flood would arrive in every region. These meters were huge tanks linked to the river by canals and underground passages. The cisterns measured variations in water levels, and recorded the minimum level of the water.

PERET (EMERGENCE)

From mid-November to mid-March the level of the waters lower. After cutting the cane and rebuilding the now worn-away banks, the farmers plough and sow the fields.

SHEMU (DROUGHT)

From mid-March to mid-July the Nile is at its lowest. The crops are picked in time for the harvesting and selling of corn and flax.

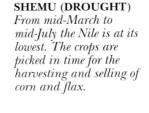

WATER CLOCKS

The Egyptians invented a primitive waterclock, which could show the time even in the sun's absence. The clepsydra was a pot, filled to the brim with water, but with holes in its base. The water leaked through the holes, and the water level gradually went down, showing the passing of time (see pages 22-3).

THE FARMERS' CALENDAR

The Pleiades (a cluster of stars) appear

The crane emigrates

The leaves fall

From the beginning of time peasant farmers, although not astronomers or mathematicians, drew up various calendars. These were precise and detailed. They were not often written down: generally they were handed down by word of mouth. Farming life was based on the observation of nature – the sky, climate changes and plant and animal behaviour – and work was organised into the different seasons of the year. Knowledge was handed down from generation to generation, and is still in use today in country areas. Before 700 BC the Greek poet, Hesiod, composed his major poem, *Works and Days*. The second part of this poem describes the country farming year in great detail, and shows the type of work suitable for each season.

A TIME FOR EVERYTHING
Along the bottom of these two pages you will see pictures of activities such as navigation, seed sowing and moving the animals. Above these are illustrations of the natural events, such as the appearance of certain stars, which helped the farmer do the right work at the right time.

Arthur appears

The swallows arrive

Autumnal rains

Start of winter rains

Winds and snow

Winter solstice

Ploughing starts

Ploughing and pruning of vines

Boats are taken out of the water

Animals are brought under cover

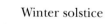

May ploughing

OCTOBER   NOVEMBER   DECEMBER   JANUARY   FEBRUARY   MARCH

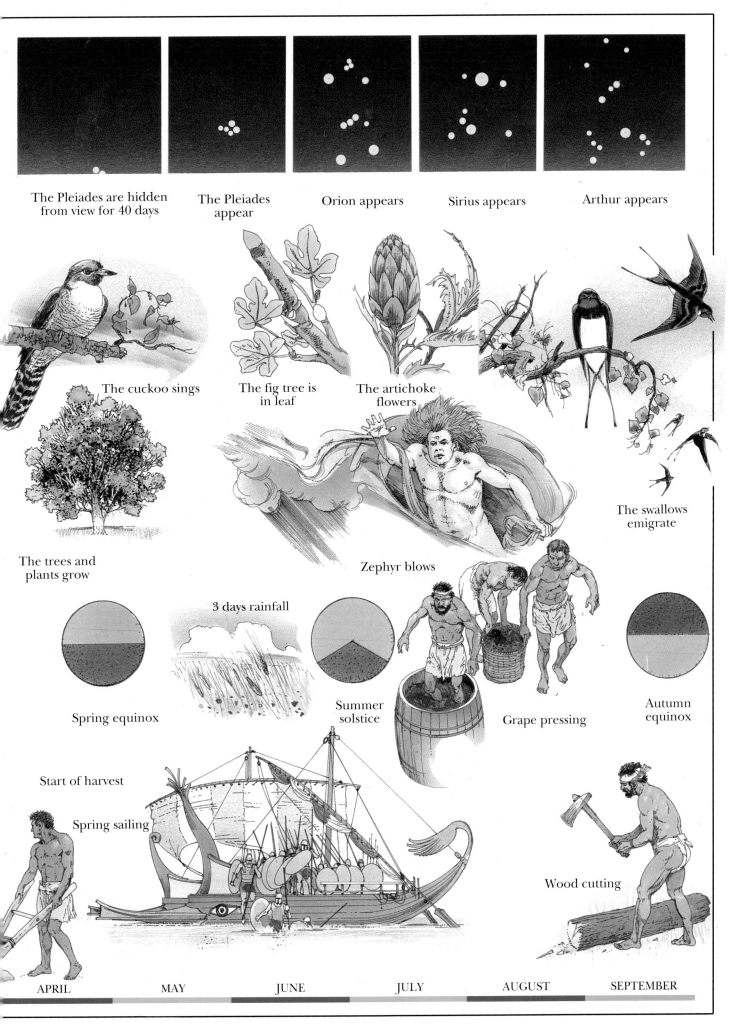

The Pleiades are hidden from view for 40 days

The Pleiades appear

Orion appears

Sirius appears

Arthur appears

The cuckoo sings

The fig tree is in leaf

The artichoke flowers

The swallows emigrate

The trees and plants grow

Zephyr blows

3 days rainfall

Spring equinox

Summer solstice

Grape pressing

Autumn equinox

Start of harvest

Spring sailing

Wood cutting

APRIL   MAY   JUNE   JULY   AUGUST   SEPTEMBER

OUR CALENDAR

It is not easy to design a calendar which will last and which is regular. The main problem is in joining the solar year, which has just over 365 days, with the lunar month, which is 29.5 days. 29.5 does not go into 365 without leaving a remainder. The Romans found an easy solution. They stopped using the moon and divided the year into 12: 12 months of 30 or 31 days, except one of 28 (or 29 every leap-year). This calendar was called the Roman, or Julian, calendar.

Our calendar is based on the Julian calendar, and was drawn up in 1582 by Pope Gregory XIII. He needed to correct a small error made by Roman astronomers: the Julian year was 11 minutes and 14 seconds longer than the actual solar one. 10 days too many, which had been building up until the point of Pope Gregory's new calendar, were removed. The day that would have been October 5, 1582, became October 15. It was decided that February should not have an extra day in century years that cannot be exactly divided by 400 (eg 1700 or 1800). Today the Gregorian calendar is used almost everywhere. The Julian calendar, however, survived in some countries up to 50 years ago, and there are at least 40 different calendars still in use throughout the world.

JULIUS CAESAR
(100 - 44 BC)
The Roman calendar is called Julian because it was devised for Julius Caesar (by Sosigenes).

SOSIGENES
(Ist century BC)
Alexandrian astronomer who drew up the Julian calendar. By 46 BC, the old calendar had become about three months ahead of the seasons, with winter taking place in September! Sosigenes corrected this by adding three months to the year 46 BC, which then lasted 445 days!

GREGORY XIII
(1508-1585)
It was not an accident that a pope reformed the calendar. While a delay of 10 days did not greatly affect daily life, it made the date of Easter uncertain, something which a pope would not be happy about!

EPIPHANY

EASTER SUNDAY

Romulus and Remus, the twin symbols of the foundation of Rome.

CHRONICLES
Every culture counts the years from a date it thinks is very important. The Romans count them from the foundation of Rome in 753 BC. The Jews count them from 3761 BC, the mythical date of the world's creation. The Muslims take their date as 16 July, 622 AD, the day of Mohammed's flight from Mecca. Christians count the years from the birth of Christ.

FESTIVE CALENDAR
The Christian calendar was at one time very important in everyday life. This painting, *Battle Between Carnival and Lent*, by the Flemish artist, Peter Bruegel (1526-1569), shows the complete cycle of holy ceremonies, with their different rites and customs.

PALM SUNDAY

MARDI GRAS
(SHROVE TUESDAY)

THE RULE OF ROME

Under Julius Caesar, Rome became a huge Empire, stretching all over the Mediterranean basin. Caesar realised that a standard time system was necessary for the good running of the state.

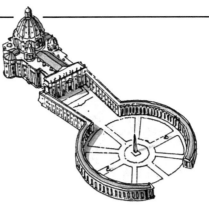

THE SPREAD OF THE GREGORIAN CALENDAR
1582

Catholic countries such as France, Italy, Spain and Portugal quickly accepted the new calendar.

1700

Protestant countries refused to adopt the calendar until 1700. For over a century they preferred to be at odds with the sun rather than in agreement with a pope.

1752

When the new calendar was put into force in England, it was necessary to remove 11 days from September. There was almost a civil war with people publicly shouting: 'Give us back the days you have robbed'.

1873

The Gregorian calendar was introduced to Japan. The years, though, are still counted from 660 BC, the legendary date of the Empire's foundation.

HOLY WEEK

CANDLEMAS

1918

The calendar was adopted in Russia only after the 1918 revolution. 13 days had to be got rid of. So according to our calendar the October revolution really took place in November!

LENT

SHROVETIDE

OTHER CALENDARS

The Gregorian calendar is the only calendar which is based completely on the sun. All other calendars, from the ancient Chinese and Aztec, to the Jewish and Islamic ones, are lunar based or both lunar and solar. One of the reasons for the popularity of the lunar based calendar is that the moon's cycle can be seen in a relatively short time – 29.5 days – while it takes one year for the sun cycle to occur.

THE WAILING WALL
Jews praying at the wailing wall in Jerusalem. The wall forms part of the remains of the ancient Temple of Solomon.

A NEOLITHIC CALENDAR
This 30,000 year-old bone tablet may be humankind's first written calendar. To an inexpert eye the signs seem accidental. The American scholar Marshack, however, looking at them through a microscope, discovered that they are in groups of 29 or 30. These seemed to stand for the days in a lunar month. Marshack guessed it was a type of almanac. If this is true, then these bone tablets are also the first examples of writing – where a sign equals a thing.

SAMARRA
9th century minaret (the turret of a mosque) from Samarra, Iraq.

THE JEWISH CALENDAR
This is very old and is now only used for religious festivals. It appeared in the 4th century AD in its existing form and is a lunar-solar calendar: the months follow the phases of the moon, while the year is solar. To help the lunar and solar year fit together comfortably, the months are alternately 30 and 29 days long. In addition, seven times in every 19 year period, an extra 29 day month is added. The names of the months are Assyrian-Babylonian, and derive from the time of Jewish slavery in the 6th century BC. Except for Saturday, the days have no names, but are simply called 'the first' (our Sunday), 'the second', and so on, day of the week.

THE ISLAMIC CALENDAR
This is one of the few modern lunar calendars. The Islamic year is the sum of 12 lunations. It only has 354 days and is, therefore, shorter than the Gregorian year. According to the Koran, the month begins when the first crescent of the new moon becomes visible. Many Islamic farmers and shepherds still follow this rule. Around the time of the new moon they watch the sky where the sun has set, waiting to see the moon. City people, though, use calendars calculated and written like ours.

MESOAMERICAN CALENDARS

The Maya and the Aztecs counted time in a similar way to each other, using two calendars. The religious one was 260 days, divided into 13 'months' of 20 days. The farming one, though, followed the solar year. It was divided into 18 months of 20 days, to which 5 'unfavourable' days were added. Every 52 years was the time of 'threat' when it was thought the world could end. To stop this, the Aztecs put out all the fires in their temples and houses, praying that the gods would allow the earth to last for another cycle.

COPAN HONDURAS. The levelling of the temples in the 8th century.

PEKING Pagoda of perpetual harmony, the Forbidden City. Ming dynasty (1368-1644)

THE CHINESE CALENDAR

The ancient Chinese adopted a lunar-solar calendar. This consisted of 12 lunar months. Every so often a thirteenth was added, to keep up with the sun and seasonal cycles. The years were grouped in eras, similar to our centuries, but were only 60 years in length. The calendars were sacred documents. They were drawn up in great secret at court and presented every year to the citizens during special ceremonies. They revealed the emperor's divine power, and showed he could foretell the future and control nature.

THE PERFECT CALENDAR

In the 1950s a group of US scholars put forward an idea to make the Gregorian calendar simpler. By getting rid of the 365th day, the year can be divided into four equal parts or quarters, each quarter having one 31 day month and two months of 30 days. 364 is also divisible by 7, leaving no remainders, so every year would have the same number of weeks – 52. They suggested that the 365th day should be used as an annual World Day, dedicated to friendship between peoples. This idea was approved by the UN as well as by the Vatican. So far, however, nothing has been done about it.

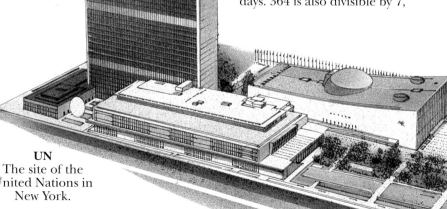

UN The site of the United Nations in New York.

THE SOLAR CLOCK

As activities such as trade and crafts developed alongside agriculture, our ancestors needed to measure time more accurately than before. The natural divisions of night and day were no longer precise enough. Early peoples began to divide the day into equal parts, or hours. To measure them, they used the simplest and most natural clock available: the sun.

We have all noticed how the shadow of any object changes position throughout the day. The solar clock made use of this fact. The clock was made up of a dial, marked with the hours of the day, and a rod (called a gnomon). As the sun moved across the sky, the shadow would fall over the different markings and show the time. The sundial of Campo Marzio, declared finished by the Emperor Augustus in 9 BC, has an obelisk from Heliopolis as its gnomon.

the obelisk point casts its shadow precisely

line of shadow at winter solstice

line of shadow to the equinoxes

mosaics with astronomical symbols and other writings

THE OBELISK OF AUGUSTUS
This was originally erected in Heliopolis, Egypt, in the 6th century BC by the Pharoah, Psamtik III. It is a single large block made of porphyry (a hard rock quarried in ancient Egypt). It is 22 m high and 3 m wide, and it weighs more than 250 tons. Its four sides celebrate in hieroglyphics the Pharoah's deeds. In 1792 it was restored by Pope Pius VI and re-erected in Rome.

EGYPTIAN OBELISKS
Another 11 obelisks were taken to Rome and placed in the main squares. The popularity of these enormous stones, was widespread: in the 19th century other obelisks were taken to London, New York and Paris. The ones in London and New York are known as Cleopatra's Needles.

SUNDIALS
Monumental sundials were not just built because of the fashion of making big things. The great height of the gnomon made the shadow's daily steps very obvious, showing the date as well as the hour.

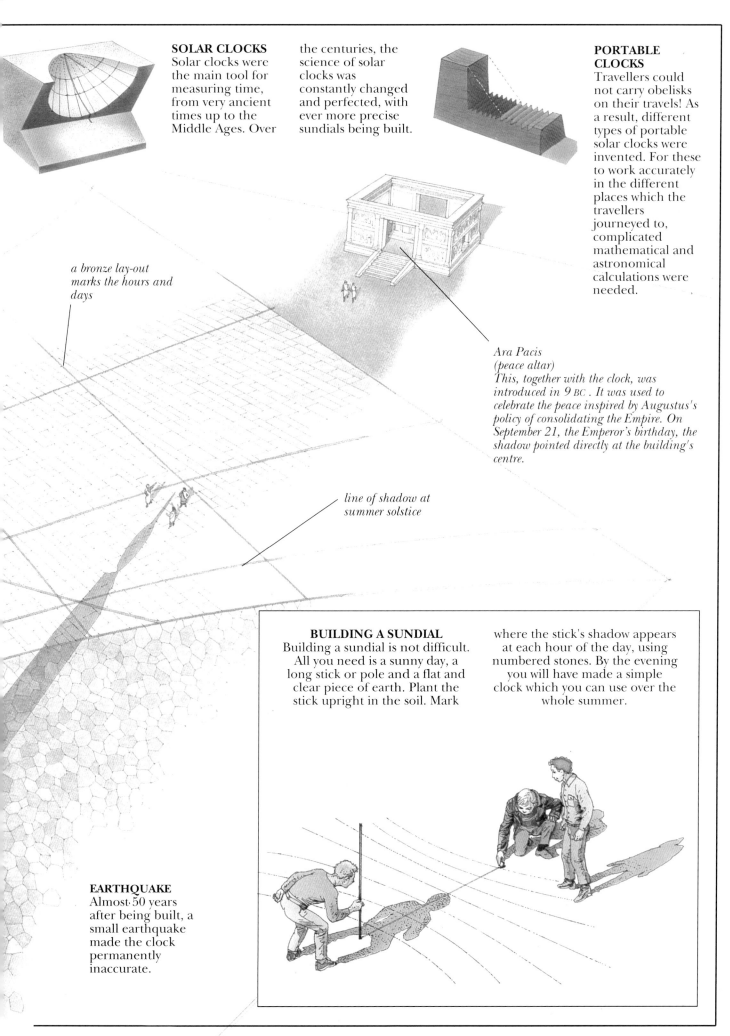

SOLAR CLOCKS
Solar clocks were the main tool for measuring time, from very ancient times up to the Middle Ages. Over the centuries, the science of solar clocks was constantly changed and perfected, with ever more precise sundials being built.

PORTABLE CLOCKS
Travellers could not carry obelisks on their travels! As a result, different types of portable solar clocks were invented. For these to work accurately in the different places which the travellers journeyed to, complicated mathematical and astronomical calculations were needed.

a bronze lay-out marks the hours and days

*Ara Pacis
(peace altar)
This, together with the clock, was introduced in 9 BC. It was used to celebrate the peace inspired by Augustus's policy of consolidating the Empire. On September 21, the Emperor's birthday, the shadow pointed directly at the building's centre.*

line of shadow at summer solstice

BUILDING A SUNDIAL
Building a sundial is not difficult. All you need is a sunny day, a long stick or pole and a flat and clear piece of earth. Plant the stick upright in the soil. Mark where the stick's shadow appears at each hour of the day, using numbered stones. By the evening you will have made a simple clock which you can use over the whole summer.

EARTHQUAKE
Almost 50 years after being built, a small earthquake made the clock permanently inaccurate.

WATER CLOCKS

Solar clocks have extremely refined systems which allow time to be measured very precisely. They also, though, have two great enemies: night and cloud. Ways of telling the time without using the sun were always being looked for. One of the oldest and simplest solutions was the clepsydra. The reason for its name – clepsydra or 'waterthief' – is that it allowed time to be measured by the slow leaking out of water through holes in the bottom of the pot (see page 13).

Later, the Greeks completely reworked the clepsydra. They used the force of the water to move complex and reliable clocks, such as the Tower of the Winds in Athens. However, even this invention had its disadvantages. Water is often full of impurities and lime. With time, the build-up of limescale slowed down the flow of water, or even completely clogged up the narrow pipes. Another problem was that, during winter, a simple frost was enough to stop the clock from working.

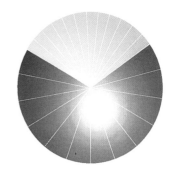

WINTER

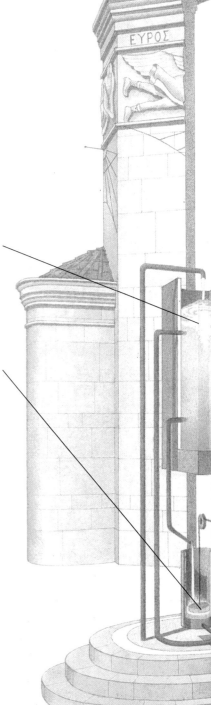

THE TOWER OF THE WINDS
This was built in Athens by the architect Andronicus of Cyrrhus in the 1st century BC. Its name is derived from its octagonal sides, which face the direction of the eight main winds. Inside the tower there was a water clock.

TOYS
The water clock, like many other clever Greek inventions, was thought of as a toy rather than as a useful instrument.

a huge tank filled with water from the Acropolis hill

the float is tied to a small chain with a counterweight, which makes the clock's disc turn

THE CLOCK OF CTESIBIUS
This was invented in the 3rd century BC. Water is directed through a narrow tube into a tank. As the water level inside the tank rises, it pushes up a huge float carrying a statuette. The finger of the moving statuette points to marks on a cylinder, indicating each passing hour of the day or night.

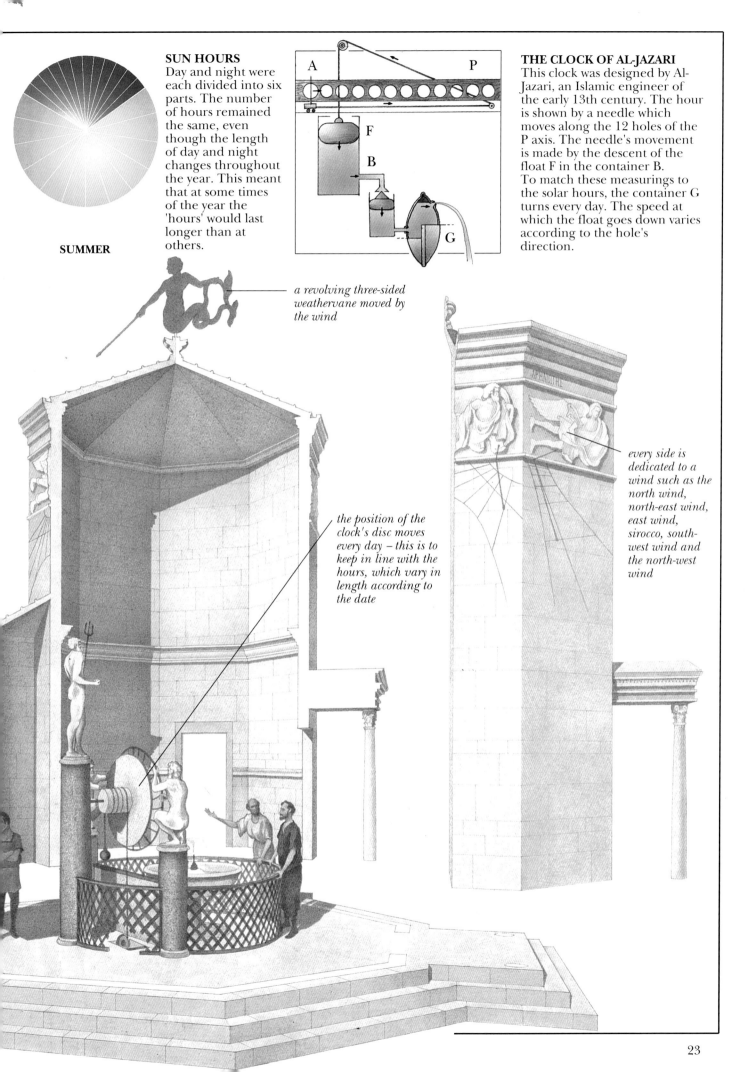

SUN HOURS

Day and night were each divided into six parts. The number of hours remained the same, even though the length of day and night changes throughout the year. This meant that at some times of the year the 'hours' would last longer than at others.

SUMMER

THE CLOCK OF AL-JAZARI

This clock was designed by Al-Jazari, an Islamic engineer of the early 13th century. The hour is shown by a needle which moves along the 12 holes of the P axis. The needle's movement is made by the descent of the float F in the container B. To match these measurings to the solar hours, the container G turns every day. The speed at which the float goes down varies according to the hole's direction.

a revolving three-sided weathervane moved by the wind

the position of the clock's disc moves every day – this is to keep in line with the hours, which vary in length according to the date

every side is dedicated to a wind such as the north wind, north-east wind, east wind, sirocco, south-west wind and the north-west wind

ASTROLABE
(11th century)
This was used by the ancient Greeks. The Arabs adopted it, making it simpler and more accurate.

ARAB ASTROLABE
(14th century)
The lever was used to point to the stars.

THE ARABS AND THE ASTROLABE

The West did not immediately develop the inventions of the Greeks. It was the Arabs who inherited the knowledge and the technology to take the inventions further. The Arabs were great mathematicians and astronomers: they were the first to divide the day into 24 hours, each hour lasting the same amount of time, no matter what the time of year. The hours were measured with complex and accurate water clocks.

The Arabs also invented the first reliable instruments to work out the geographic position and local time at sea. Such instruments were then used for exploring and trading throughout the world. In little more than a century – between the 7th and 8th – the Arabs conquered a wide area from Iran to the edge of Christian Europe, an area including the African Mediterranean coasts and the Iberian peninsular.

HOW THE ASTROLABE WORKS

The astrolabe is made of a flat disc to which various circular plates are attached. These relate to the position of parallels and meridians. A perforated sheet, reproducing the position of the stars, is then hinged onto these. By focusing on the chosen star and by moving the discs, it is possible to determine one's position in relation to the horizon.

THE KAIROUAN MOSQUE
The first mosque, built in North Africa in the 7th century, was a simple enclosure facing Mecca. The present building is the fifth mosque to be built on a site dating from Aghlabid times.

ARAB ASTROLABE
(14th century)
The inscriptions are in both Hebrew and in Arabic.

KAIROUAN MOSQUE
Inside the Kairouan mosque's prayer room, there are 500 columns made up from Roman and Byzantine monuments.

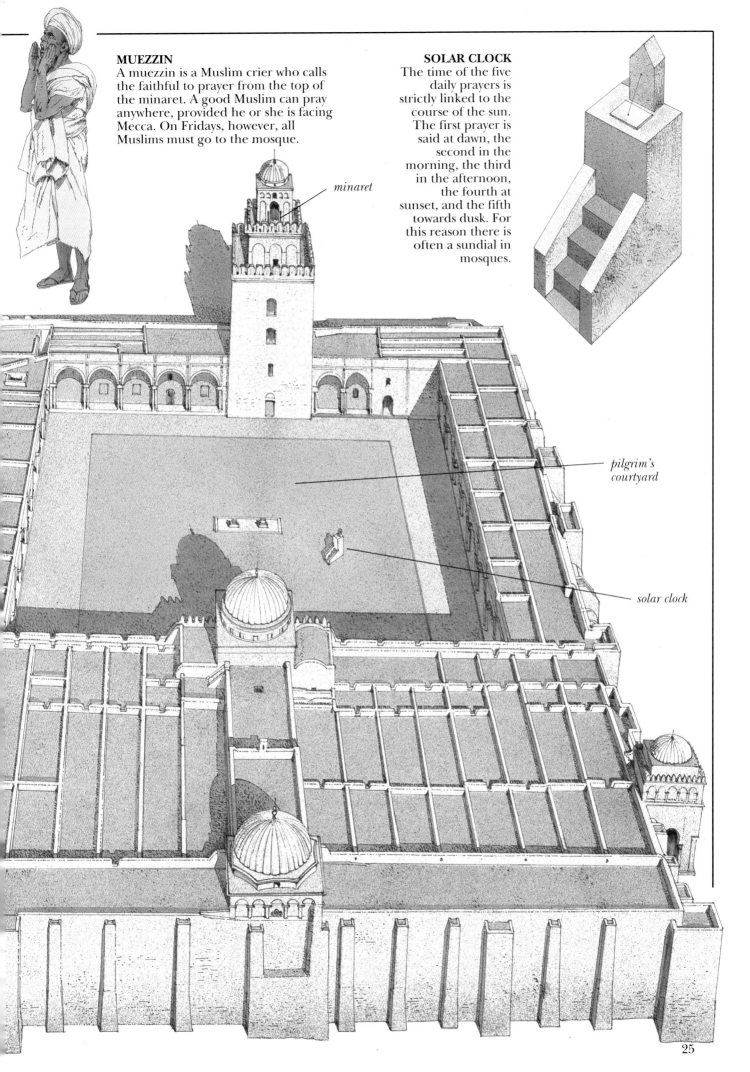

MUEZZIN

A muezzin is a Muslim crier who calls the faithful to prayer from the top of the minaret. A good Muslim can pray anywhere, provided he or she is facing Mecca. On Fridays, however, all Muslims must go to the mosque.

minaret

SOLAR CLOCK

The time of the five daily prayers is strictly linked to the course of the sun. The first prayer is said at dawn, the second in the morning, the third in the afternoon, the fourth at sunset, and the fifth towards dusk. For this reason there is often a sundial in mosques.

pilgrim's courtyard

solar clock

THE SOUND OF TIME

In the 6th century AD the monk Benedict founded a new religious order. Benedictine rules were based on a simple motto: 'ora et labora', pray and work. Many well-organised and productive small-town monasteries were set up across medieval western Europe. These communities needed a uniform, accurate and, most importantly, public system of time. Because of this, the bell was introduced to organise the monks and to call them to their different duties. The tolling of the bell told the monks when to pray, and divided the day into periods of work, study and rest. Up to the 13th century, the bells were rung according to time read on sundials and clepsydras. With technological progress, these basic methods were soon replaced by the first mechanical clocks.

The refectory. In the summer and on Sundays two meals were eaten: the main meal at the sixth hour (midday) and a light one after the ninth (about 6 o' clock). In winter there was only one meal.

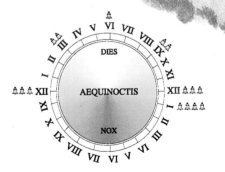

mill

barn

oven

gardens

cemetery

The counterweights allow the speed to increase or decrease, so the clock is in time with the solar hours.

foliot

rod

rim teeth

the dial rotates while the hand remains fixed

weight

MECHANICAL CLOCKS

The first of these were simple counterweight mechanisms – a weight made the face rotate or the hand move. The great improvement in the mechanical clock consisted in the 'escapement', which made the clock's movement regular. The rim teeth beat on the rod, and the foliot made sure the release movement was smooth.

DIES

AEQUINOCTIS

NOX

CANONICAL HOURS

The day was divided into set times for prayer, varying in length according to the season: the first 'hour'(dawn); the third(mid-morning); the sixth (midday); the ninth (mid-afternoon); the twelfth(sunset). To these were added three nightly times for prayer: compline (after sunset); matins (midnight); and laude (an hour before dawn).

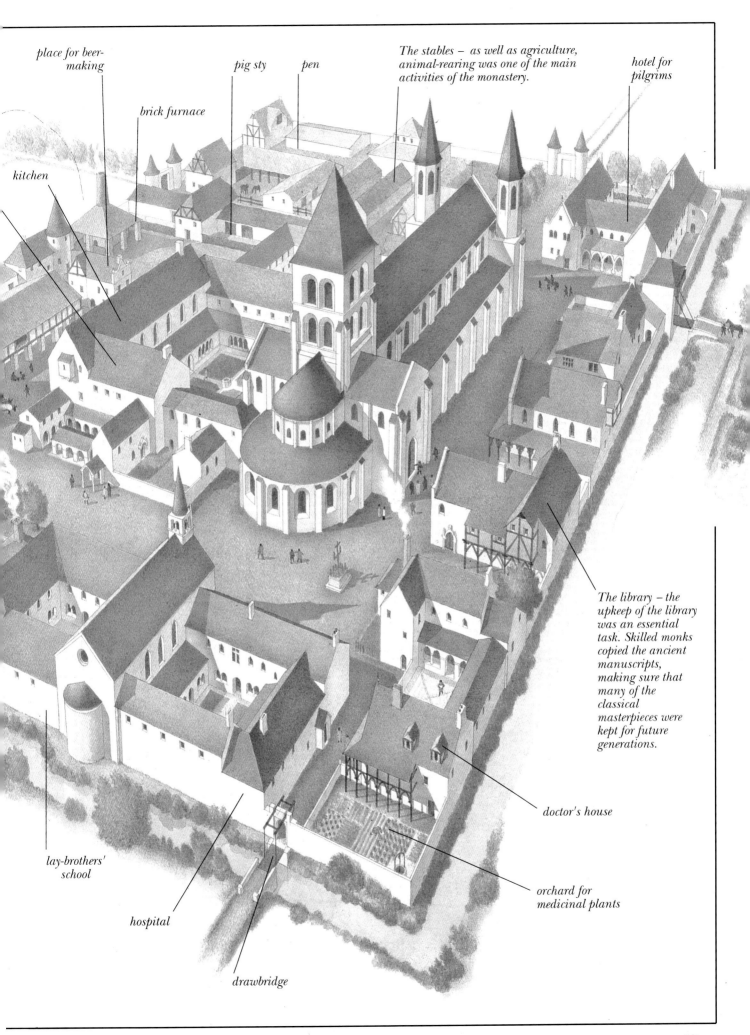

place for beer-making

brick furnace

pig sty

pen

The stables – as well as agriculture, animal-rearing was one of the main activities of the monastery.

hotel for pilgrims

kitchen

The library – the upkeep of the library was an essential task. Skilled monks copied the ancient manuscripts, making sure that many of the classical masterpieces were kept for future generations.

doctor's house

lay-brothers' school

hospital

drawbridge

orchard for medicinal plants

TIME IN THE CITY

Invented in the monasteries, the mechanical clock arrived in the city in the 14th century. This was a time of great economic and political change. The city tower, with its clock became an essential tool. The time shown on the clock decided what pace the new artisan and trading activities should go at, a pace much faster than that of previous centuries. It also marked the moments typical of city life: the opening and closing of the city gates, the changes of the guard, when the market was open and the times of meetings.

The mechanical clock showed how successful it was when, at the end of the century, most western cities decided not to use the unequal solar hours. They chose, instead, a day divided into 12 equal parts.

THE STUDENT
The student of this period would get up before dawn. Lessons started at six and were made up of reading texts. Shorter lessons, revisions and repetitions began at nine o'clock. After midday lunch, the teacher's questions would be discussed. The sudent would end the day by meeting friends for a drink in the tavern.

THE CITY CLOCK
City clocks were not only useful for telling the citizens the time – in fact, many clocks were inaccurate. Just as important, was the fact that each city clock represented its city. Public clocks had to be handsome and unusual. Today we can still see very beautiful clocks in the major European cities, such as the ones in Prague's Town Hall (above) and the tower of St Mark's, Venice, (below), both from the 15th century.

the change of the guards

the city gates

THE ARTISAN
The artisan worked at home, often with the whole family helping him. He got up at dawn and worked until midday, when he would eat. After a short rest, he worked until the evening. Working at night was forbidden but, if necessary, artisans sometimes would finish an urgent task in secret.

THE WORKMAN
The first labourers for the cloth industry worked hard the whole day. They laboured from dawn till dusk, only taking a short lunch break at midday. To round up his low pay, a workman often asked for overtime. He worked until curfew and finished his day by going to bed early.

THE MERCHANT
The day began at dawn for the merchant, at which time he would wake and go to his shop. At midday he returned home for public duties or social reasons. He would write letters, meet relatives, arrange marriages and take part in business meetings. In the evening he read and chatted at home.

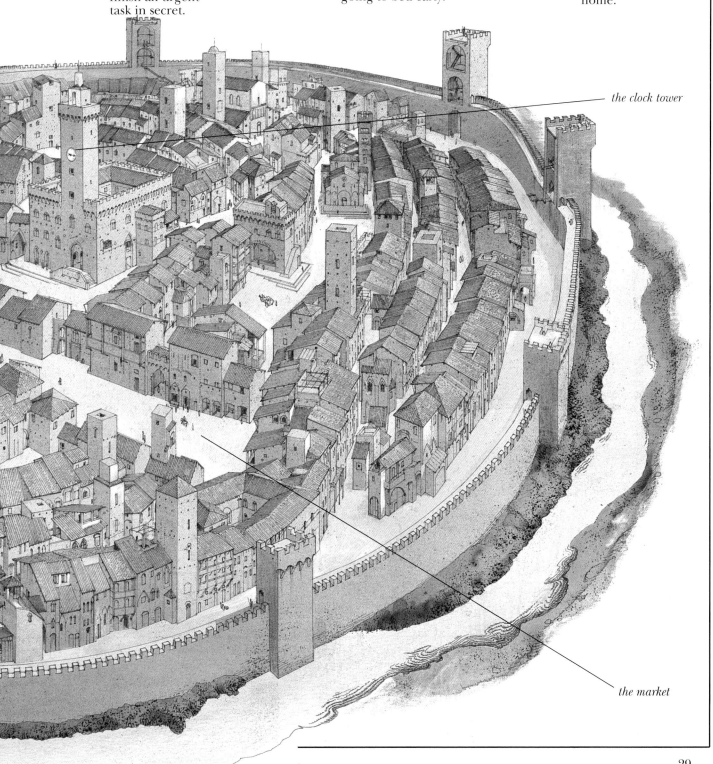

the clock tower

the market

**GALILEO GALILEI
(1564-1642)**
In 1610 Galileo proved that Copernicus was right: the sun did not revolve round the earth. Instead, the earth revolved around the sun. The church would not accept this discovery, which was against all their teaching. They imprisoned Galileo, and forced him to tell the world that his ideas were wrong.

THE TIME OF SCIENCE

The 17th century was the age of the first modern scientists. Galileo, Kepler, Descartes and Newton were talented scholars who began to study the world in a new way. They no longer simply accepted the views of the church or of 'tradition'. Instead, they wanted to look at and measure nature in a scientific way. The situation arose where reliable instruments for making accurate observations were needed.

The most important of these instruments were those for measuring time. Although, by this date, clocks were accurate enough for everyday life, they were completely useless in scientific experiments. They were imprecise and very basic, showing only hours, not minutes or seconds. Often the scientists invented and made their own instruments for their experiments, for example the pendulum clock and the telescope. Even today, many scientists must invent the complicated equipment which they use in their own experiments.

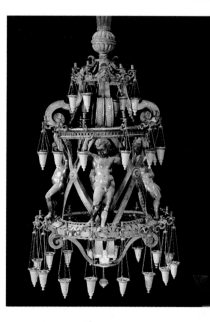

THE LAMP OF PISA CATHEDRAL
According to legend, Galileo watched this huge lamp swinging in the wind. As he watched, he noticed how the time it took for the lamp to swing from one side to the other was always the same, no matter the size of the swing.

**CHRISTIAAN HUYGENS
(1629-1695)**
In 1655, using a lens he himself had built, Huygens discovered Saturn's first satellite. Huygens is most famous, however, for his clocks. These made use of Galileo's pendulum theories.

THE PENDULUM CLOCK
When the pendulum swings to the left, its little ball lifts the stop and the runged wheel can turn. The wheel continues to turn until another rung is blocked by a second little ball. When the pendulum swings to the right the rung is freed by the second little ball. The first ball then blocks the next rung, and so the process continues.

THE PENDULUM
The time it takes for a pendulum to swing from side to side is always the same, no matter how far it swings to the right or left. This fact is called isochronism. It had already been discovered by the Arabs in the 11th century. Galileo and Huygens, however, had the clever idea of using it in clock-making.

GALILEO'S LENS TELESCOPES
These were simple lead tubes. Two lenses were placed at their ends. One of the lenses was concave and the other was convex.

THE TELESCOPE
In 1668 Isaac Newton made the first mirror telescope. It was an essential tool for studying the stars. With this, Newton could see distant objects, including those invisible to the naked eye, in great detail. The telescope had two mirrors. One mirror picked up the image, then reflected it onto a second, flat mirror. This then reflected the image to the person studying the sky.

HUMAN CLOCK
Galileo wanted to measure the speed of falling objects. Because an accurate clock had not yet been made, Galileo used a 'human clock'. This 'clock' was made up of lots of assistants who each counted their own pulse. The average number of pulses of everybody counting was worked out, and a nearly exact time was found.

NAVIGATION

Up until the 14th century, European sailors did not travel far from the coasts. They hardly ever left the Mediterranean, where it was easy to find the way using simple landmarks and a good knowledge of winds and currents. Although a basic compass had been in existence since the 11th century, around 1300 the compass was greatly improved. Voyages now became longer.

Finding out the distance travelled, however, remained a great problem. The only way to work it out it was by knowing the hour that the ship left, and comparing it with the local time where the sailors arrived. Because of this, it was very important to carry some sort of clock which could keep time over a long period, without losing or gaining minutes or hours. Travellers used simple clepsydras, but during voyages they would become slow, leading to large errors in routes. Mechanical clocks did not improve things much, since the ship's movement interfered with the movement of the clock's pendulum. The problem of finding out the length of the distance travelled was only finally solved in the 18th century, when precision sea chronometers were invented.

THE COMPASS
By the year 1300, the compass was used by both Christian and Muslim peoples in the Mediterranean. This led to great changes in travelling. As the compass always pointed north, the ship's direction could be found out night or day, whether the sky was clear or cloudy.

LATITUDE
This is the distance in degrees between parallel points. At the equator, we see the polar star on the horizon. At the north pole we see it above our heads, 90° over the horizon. Latitude, then, is easily discovered by measuring the angle of the polar star with the horizon.

LOG
A ship's speed was measured by a log. This was a simple knotted rope which was towed by a float and ran astern (behind the ship). By counting the knots during a measure of time, the speed of the ship was found out. Today, electronic instruments are used, but speed is still expressed in knots.

LONGITUDE
This is the distance in degrees between the meridians. To discover the longitude a traveller would first work out the time of the journey in hours, by comparing the local time with the place of departure's time. By then noting the boat's speed, (how far it was travelling per hour) the longitude could be worked out.

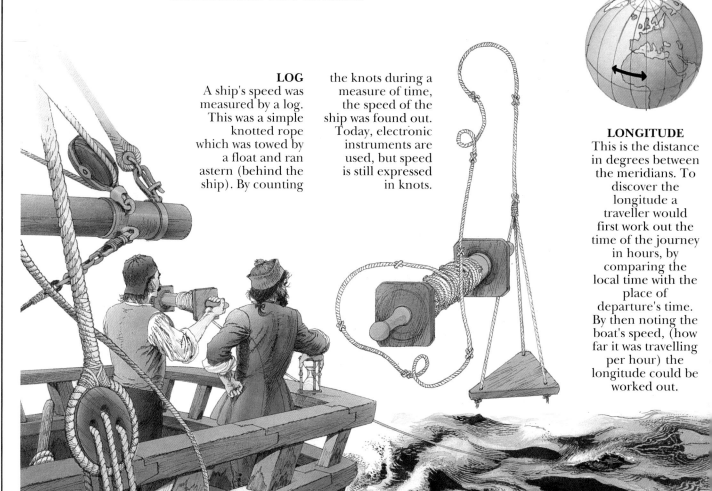

THE SEXTANT
The sextant is descended from the astrolabe. By making note of a star's height on the horizon, it is possible to find out the longitude and local time.

THE MARINE CHRONOMETER
The first efficient marine chronometers were made around 1761 by the English shipwright John Harrison. For his work, Harrison won a prize of £20,000 from the Board of Longitude, an English instituion.

CHRISTOPHER COLUMBUS 1451-1506
On his famous voyage (1502-4), Columbus was convinced he had arrived in India. He knew the earth was round, but thought it was smaller. Due to this error in calculating longitude, the land he discovered was America, not India.

CARAVEL
The first great 15th-16th century explorers carried out their voyages in small wooden boats called caravels. They could not be destroyed by storms and were made so that they could hold huge loads. The triangular sails also made use of the sideways winds which blew on the boats.

WORLD TIME

From the 16th century onwards, more and more merchants travelled long distances to trade in far off places. Although their travels were safer and faster than ever before, they were still complicated because the time was measured differently in all the places the travellers sailed to. Every country, even every city, had its own system. The day could start at midnight, midday, dawn or sunset! Travellers had to trust in long and complicated tables setting out the different time systems.

With the invention of trains in the 19th century, travelling became much quicker. The need for a 'world time' became essential. In 1884 an international commission decided to divide the world into 24 time zones, each zone using the same system of time. After long discussion, the Greenwich meridian in London was chosen as the departure point.

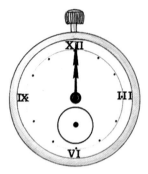

SUMMER AND WINTER TIME
To make the best use of daylight hours, many countries put their clocks forward by an hour in March, then back an hour in September.

TIME ZONES
The Greenwich meridian is at 0°. Each successive zone is changed by one hour. One hour is added to each zone going eastward, and subtracted from each zone going westward. To keep things simple, it was decided that where a large part of a country was in a certain time zone, the whole country would be looked at as being in that same time zone.

THE WORLD IN 24 ZONES
The system which divided the world into 24 zones was proposed in 1859 by the Italian, Quirico Filipanti. Britain adopted the system in 1884, but Italy only in 1892.

PRECISION CLOCKS
The development of the railway led to the need for very precise clocks. The clock on the right is signed by the Danish Urban Jurgensens, heir of an old family of clockmakers.

TRAINS AND TIME
When railways were developed, many European countries still used solar time. There were different timetables, not only between countries but from city to city. The speed at which the new trains took people from place to place made these differences much more obvious, and helped people to decide to organise time in zones.

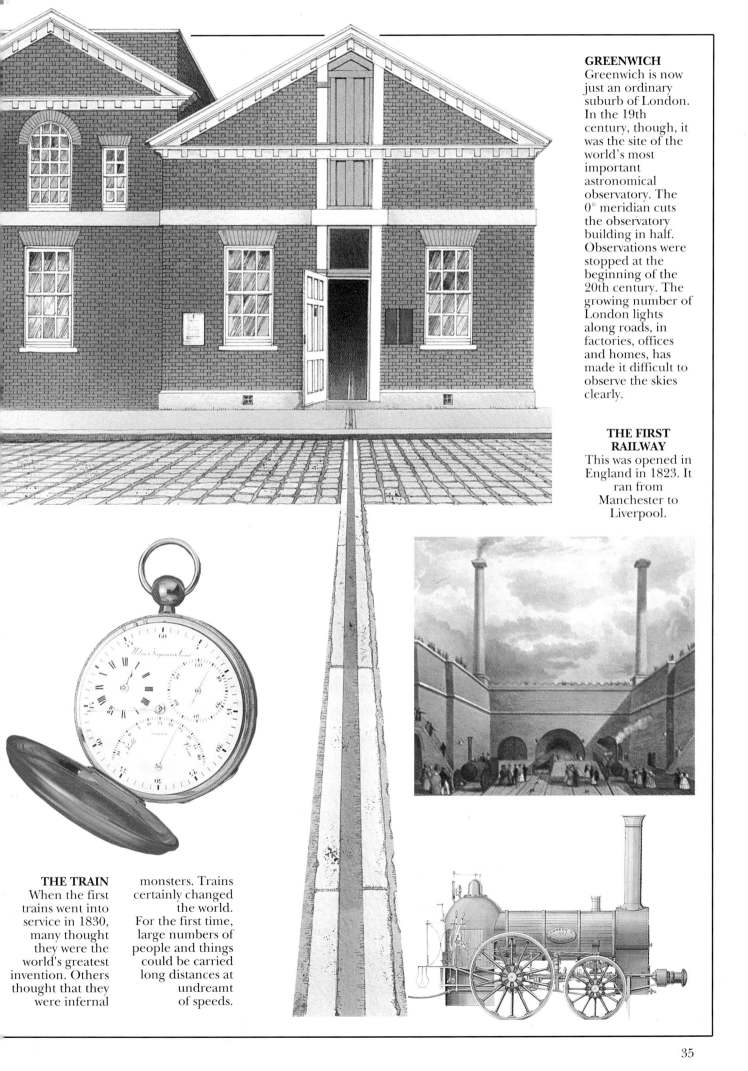

GREENWICH

Greenwich is now just an ordinary suburb of London. In the 19th century, though, it was the site of the world's most important astronomical observatory. The 0° meridian cuts the observatory building in half. Observations were stopped at the beginning of the 20th century. The growing number of London lights along roads, in factories, offices and homes, has made it difficult to observe the skies clearly.

THE FIRST RAILWAY

This was opened in England in 1823. It ran from Manchester to Liverpool.

THE TRAIN

When the first trains went into service in 1830, many thought they were the world's greatest invention. Others thought that they were infernal monsters. Trains certainly changed the world. For the first time, large numbers of people and things could be carried long distances at undreamt of speeds.

WORK TIME

The end of 18th century England saw the start of something which completely changed the world: the Industrial Revolution. Agriculture, the most important activity of every country all over the world, was now replaced by industry. First steam, then electric and oil machines, were invented. Many of the jobs which people used to do were no longer needed. Objects were now made by machines, instead of by hand. Goods were made in a fraction of the time they had been made in before.

The price for this, however, was that the lives of millions of people were completely changed. From the Industrial Revolution onwards, machines decided the work pattern of labourers, calling them to start and stop work together at the sound of the siren. Factory workers were expected to act like clockwork, ruled by the rhythm of the machines. They had to do repetitive work quickly and carefully, watched by supervisors who checked and timed every movement.

WORKING AT HOME
It was common in the 18th century in the textile industry to work from home. This type of work earnt the contractors a lot of money, and gave peasant families some extra money to live on. The whole family was employed. The men worked the loom, the women spun and the children wound the reels.

THE JACQUARD LOOM
The mechanical loom was invented by Jacquard and patented in 1804. Textile patterns were programmed onto cards with punched holes which controlled the machine. Only one worker was needed to operate the loom.

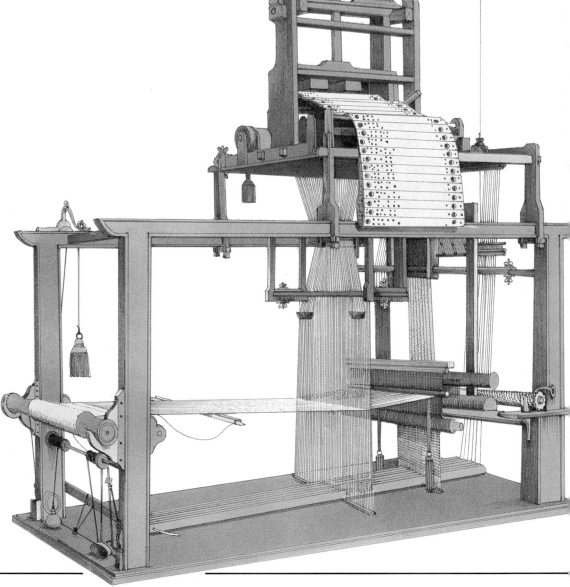

THE SPINNING MILL
The new mechanical looms invented in the Industrial Revolution were expensive and took up a lot of space. Because of this, work was moved outside the home to special buildings or factories. Mechanisation made the work much simpler. Children were often employed as they cost less and were more obedient.

THE LENGTH OF THE WORKING DAY
From the start of the Industrial Revolution, up to the present day, workers have fought to be given a more bearable and 'humane' work day. In the early 19th century, the average work day in an English textile factory was 12-13 hours! A century of strikes and demands were needed in order to get today's eight-hour day.

TIME AND MOTION STUDIES
The industrialist Henry Ford (1863-1947) was the first to adapt the work theories of Frederick Taylor (1856-1915). Ford looked at each step necessary in making a factory object. The worker's every movement was studied, and rules on the quickest times a worker took were found.

ASSEMBLY LINE
The pace of work was speeded up even more in the twenties. This was when the assembly line was introduced in the US. A conveyor belt passed the different pieces of the item being made in front of the workers. Each worker had one job only, which was repeated, over and over again!

MODERN TIMES
Charlie Chaplin, in the film *Modern Times* (1936), criticised the way that factories were organised. The film showed that factories were more concerned with the needs of the machines than with people's needs.

THE PORTABLE CLOCK

Today, all our everyday actions – catching the train, going to school or work, meeting friends – are timed very exactly. Many people wear watches and look at them constantly throughout the day. The process of reducing the size of clocks, and making them as portable as watches, has been long and difficult. An important step in this direction was the replacement of the clock's weight by a spring. By the 17th century many more clocks were being made than earlier, but they were still expensive and, as a result, were used by the rich. From then to the present day, the number of people able to own clocks has dramatically increased, thanks to more and more improvements bringing the prices down.

PORTABLE CLOCKS
The first portable clocks took up a lot of space and were heavy, as can be seen in these two examples from the 16th century.

CLOCK WITH SPRINGS
The spring balance is made from a small fly-wheel fixed to the centre of the clock case. The fly-wheel is free to rotate on itself, and is attached to a coiled spring, which in turn is connected to the clock. The fly-wheel swings, rotating the hour, and in doing so winds or unwinds the spring. Tightening or unrolling the spring can make the clock go faster or slower. Clockmakers do this to regulate inaccurate clocks.

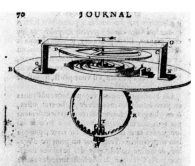

THE BALANCE
A letter from Christiaan Huygens, 1674, explaining how the spring balance works.

THE POCKET WATCH
From the 18th century onwards, the pocket watch was an essential part of a gentleman's clothing. It was connected to a chain and put in the pocket of a waistcoat. Such a watch was a sign of wealth and importance.

WATCHES OR JEWELS?

The first watches were designed as pieces of jewellery rather than as useful instruments, and they were not accurate. Here is an example of a French watch from 1640.

THE MOST COMPLICATED WATCH

This is the Swiss watch, Patek Philippe. It has 24 hands and 40 functions. These include calculating Easter Sunday, the time of dawn or sunset, and the direction of the Milky Way.

THE SWATCH WATCH

With its incredibly low price and jazzy designs, the Swatch has made watch-buying fun. Collecting the many highly-coloured different types of Swatch watches has become very fashionable.

THE POCKET WATCH AND THE WRIST WATCH

Up until World War I the wrist watch remained an unusual extravagence. Its success, however, was confirmed during the War: while under enemy fire in the trenches, soldiers found it was easier and safer to take a quick look at their wrists, rather than taking a watch out of their pockets.

SPORT

Time, and how it is measured, has a central role in sport. In many sports the length of a game is controlled by it. Football has two halves of 45 minutes; American football has four periods of 15 minutes; basketball has two periods of 20. All fans know that the victory or defeat of their team often depends on a handful of minutes or even seconds. Many individual sports are a real race against time. Records are measured in hundredths of seconds, and great victories that have passed into history are often won by mere thousandths. To measure this, sport uses complicated machinery, as elaborate and precise as the equipment used in scientific research.

STARTING OFF
It is essential that in speed competitions athletes not only set off all together but that they do so in time to the chronometer. In the last hundred years there has been steady progress in the technical side of competitions, getting ever closer to total precision.

THE FIRST SPEED COMPETITIONS
In the first speed competitions the runners ran steadily in lanes at a distance of around 4 - 6 metres from each other. Each athlete took care that competitors to the right or left did not get too close. A start line judge would decide if the line up was acceptable, only then beginning the actual race.

THE STARTING GUN
From the middle of the nineteenth century, competitions were started with a shooting pistol loaded with blanks. This gave the signal for the athletes to start and marked the moment when the chronometers should be set.

OLYMPICS
The Olympics are the world's most important sporting event, with the greatest champions and record-holders competing. The Olympic Games of the modern era were set up by the Frenchman Pierre de Fredi, Baron of Coubertin, and the first ones were held in Athens in 1876. They were derived from the Olympic Games of ancient Greece, which were held every four years in honour of Zeus.

FINISHING
An athlete has finished the race when his or her chest touches the tape. Nowadays the finishing line is made of photoelectric cells (similar to those in shop alarms). These stop the chronometer and time every athlete automatically. Before the fifties, such technology did not exist. The timing of the athletes depended on people setting off the chronometers. This was not as reliable as using machines.

JIM HINES
The American Jim Hines was the first man to break the 10 electronic second barrier in the 100 metres dash. He ran it in 9.9 seconds in the Mexican Olympics in 1968.

MANUAL AND ELECTRIC TIMINGS
In the sixties, athletic competitions were measured by two methods. One was manual: the time was measured by six chronometers and the average score was calculated from the six readings. The second was electric: readings were given by the first automatic instruments. The differences between the two methods were often very large.

ELECTRONIC VICTORY
To end the continual arguments, in 1977 the International Athletic Federation for track and field decided to use electronic times only. Some athletes were unhappy about this. They preferred the readings that manual timings gave.

PHOTOFINISH
Photoelectronic cells on the finishing lines are collected by an electric machine which films the first athletes to finish. Along with the chronometered time, this gives great accuracy in timing. The photofinish allows the finishing order to be viewed even when, to the naked eye, the athletes seem equal.

ATOMIC TIME

Up to fifty years ago the most accurate way of telling the time was the sky: the basis for working out the time was the movement of the sun, moon and the stars. The important role that astromony had in measuring time depended on the fact that the spinning of the earth around the sun was regular and unchangeable. With technological progress, however, some irregularites have been discovered. It has been calculated that in the last fifty years one second has been lost.

Recent scientists have looked for a system which is even more precise and regular than the one developed over the past centuries. In 1967 the Conference of Weights and Measures adopted a new definition of the 'second'. This new definition is based on atomic time.

THE ATOMIC CLOCK

Before the invention of the caesium atomic clock, all the instruments for measuring time depended on the swinging of a pendulum, on a balance or on quartz crystals. In 1948 scientists joined up an instrument for signalling time to an atomic vibration, creating the first atomic clock. As the atom's vibrations are independent of outside forces, time is measured in a much more exact way than by other methods. The latest atomic clocks lose only one second in a thousand years!

THE THEORY OF RELATIVITY

Early this century Albert Einstein (1879-1955) formulated the theory of relativity: 'The physical laws that we know are only valid when objects move at much slower speeds than the speed of light. When speed increases, things change dramatically.' Time provides an example of these changes, slowing down for objects travelling at almost the speed of light. A traveller moving at the speed of light would not notice any difference as long as he or she was still moving. On arrival, however, the traveller would notice that for everyone else much more time had passed than for him or herself.

THE ATOM

The atom is composed of a nucleus around which electrons move. The electrons are particles, ie, tiny pieces of material. A 1,000 billion billion are needed to make up a speck of dust. The nucleus is made of two types of particles: protons and neutrons. In all, there are 107 types of atom found in nature.

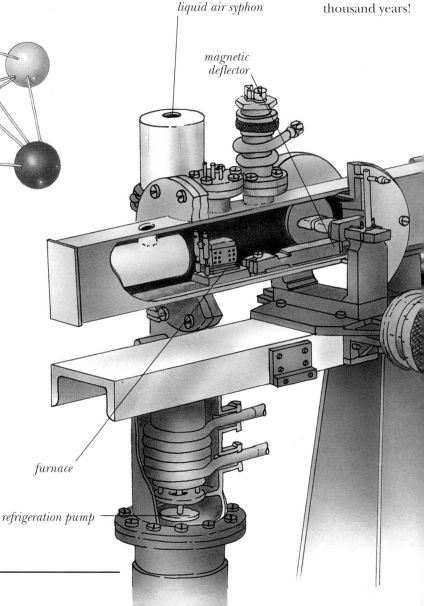

liquid air syphon

magnetic deflector

furnace

refrigeration pump

THE QUARTZ CLOCK

A compressed quartz crystal creates electricity. In the quartz clock the crystal is hit by a current, which makes the crystal vibrate. An electronic circuit changes the vibration frequency into impulses which set off the liquid crystal dial. The biggest error this type of clock can run up is 30 seconds a year. As the crystal ages, however, the frequency slows down and the clock becomes less accurate.

NAVIGATION PROBLEMS

Today's experts are still trying to help people to explore. Space ships are controlled by radar telescopes: to work out their position, the telescopes measure the time it takes for a signal to reach earth.

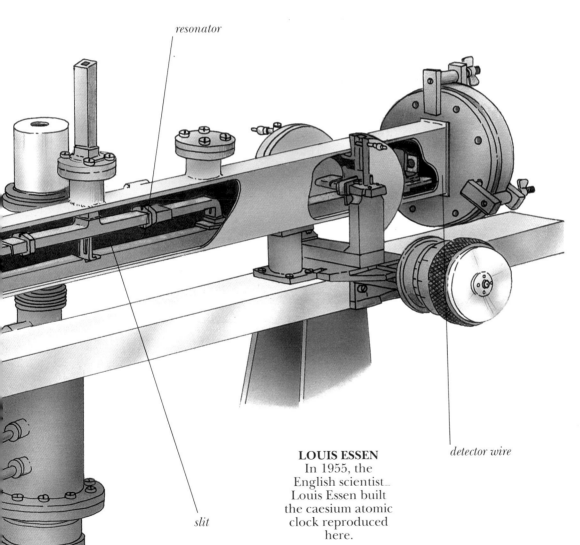

resonator

slit

detector wire

LOUIS ESSEN

In 1955, the English scientist Louis Essen built the caesium atomic clock reproduced here.

CARE OF THE ATOMIC CLOCK

Atomic clocks are operated in an underground room. They are enclosed in special cabinets, keeping them free from the smallest vibration or change in heat.

PAST TIME

Clocks and calendars measure the present and map out the future. But how are the events of the past, which happened before these tools were invented, dated? History tells us when and where things happened, but is based on written evidence: it only goes back 5,000 years, to when writing was first invented. But time is not a human invention, the years followed one another even before they were recorded. And they left traces on the earth, in the soil, in plants and bodies.

In reading such traces, a detailed story is revealed. In recent times geologists, botanists, chemists and archaeologists, each with their own different point of view, have drawn up more and more exact dating methods. We can now reconstruct the most ancient history of the earth, going back to the origin of the world and the beginning of humankind.

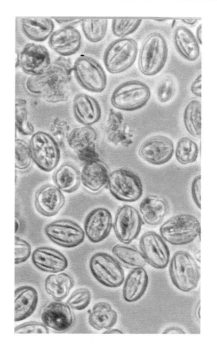

PEAT
Peat is made up of extremely old, rotten trees and plants. Hundreds and thousands of years later, we can still identify grasses and branches. By studying peat, ancient types of vegetation can be discovered and written about.

POLLEN
Pollen under the microscope. The study of pollen in peat was started by the archeologist Lennart von Post in 1916.

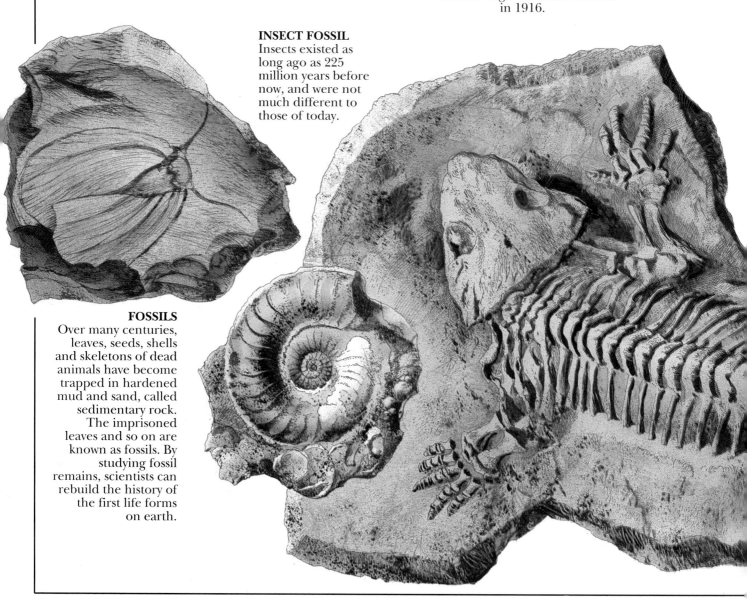

INSECT FOSSIL
Insects existed as long ago as 225 million years before now, and were not much different to those of today.

FOSSILS
Over many centuries, leaves, seeds, shells and skeletons of dead animals have become trapped in hardened mud and sand, called sedimentary rock. The imprisoned leaves and so on are known as fossils. By studying fossil remains, scientists can rebuild the history of the first life forms on earth.

DENDROCHRONOLOGY

This is the science of dating events by studying growth rings in ancient timber. You can tell a tree's age by looking at its trunk: each ring corresponds to one year. The rings are narrower in dry years and wider in wet ones. By comparing a series of pieces of wood of different ages, but from the same period of history, it is possible to go very far back in time.

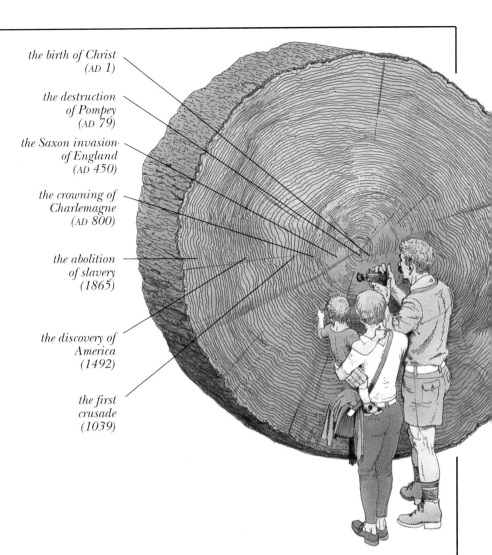

the birth of Christ (AD *1*)

the destruction of Pompey (AD *79*)

the Saxon invasion of England (AD *450*)

the crowning of Charlemagne (AD *800*)

the abolition of slavery (*1865*)

the discovery of America (*1492*)

the first crusade (*1039*)

SEQUOIA
This is a US tree which can live 2,000 years.

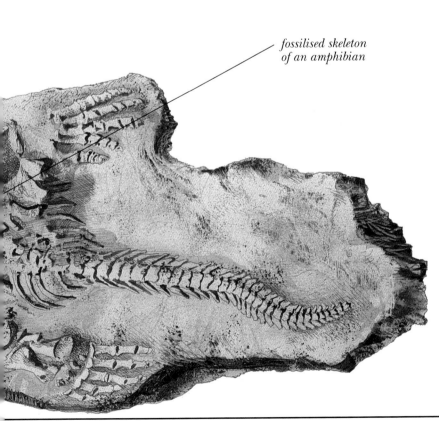

fossilised skeleton of an amphibian

HALF LIFE
The American chemist, W.F. Libby, used the carbon 14 present in organic life-forms to measure how long it takes something dead to decay. He discovered that the radiation of the carbon 14 decreased in a very slow, regular way, always halving itself at the same pace. By working out the radioactivity of organic remains, their exact age can be worked out.

EXPOSING A FORGERY!
The American egyptologist, James Breasted, asked W.F.Libby to analyse what he believed to be an ancient sarcophagus. Using carbon 14, Libby discovered that the sarcophagus was recent: it was, in fact, the work of skilful forgers!

GLOSSARY

ALMANAC A type of calendar which gives information about the positions of the stars or the movements of the tides.

ASTROLABE Astronomical instrument based on the movement of the stars. It was used by sailors to help find their position.

ASTROLOGY The study of the influence of the stars over the earth and its inhabitants.

ASTRONOMY The study of the movements of the stars and planets.

CALENDAR A system for dividing time into fixed periods, based on astronomical observations.

CANONICAL HOURS The six divisions of the day when monks pray.

CARBON 14 A radioactive element of all living beings, which slowly disintegrates after death. The age of organic remains can be found out by measuring the quantity of C 14 left.

CHRONICLES A history of past events, written in the order in which they occurred.

CHRONOMETER A type of clock, particularly one which can withstand bad weather conditions or being kept on board ship.

CLEPSYDRA A water clock which uses the regular flow of water to measure time.

COMPASS An instrument used to determine the cardinal points (North, South, East and West). It has a magnetic needle which always points North.

CURFEW In the Middle Ages this was the signal given an hour after sunset to tell people to cover their fires and put out their lights.

DAY The 24 hour period of time starting from midnight onwards (see **earth**).

DENDROCHRONOLOGY This is the science of measuring the age of trees. It is based on the number of growth rings visible on the trunk.

EARTH A satellite of the sun. It takes about 365 days to go round the sun (a year). The earth also revolves round itself – this rotation takes a day.

ECLIPSE When the sun or moon is suddenly hidden from the earth. There is an eclipse of the sun when the moon comes between the sun and the earth; there is an eclipse of the moon when the earth is positioned between the sun and the moon and throws its shadow over the moon.

EQUINOXES The spring or autumn equinox is when the length of day and night is the same throughout the world, that is, 12 hours.

ESCAPEMENT The part of mechanical clock which regulates the movement, keeping the time constant.

FOSSIL The remains of very old plants and animals, trapped in sedimentary rock.

GNOMON The rod which goes across the dial of solar clocks (see **sundial**).

HEMISPHERE One of the two halves of the world. The southern and the northern hemispheres are divided by the equator.

HORIZON The line at which the earth and sky appear to meet.

HOUR A unit of time. There are 24 hours in a day. Every hour is divided into 60 minutes, which in turn is divided into 60 seconds.

INDUSTRIAL REVOLUTION The widespread introduction of machinery into industry from the end of the 18th century. It dramatically changed the way work was done.

ISOCHRONISM The principle set out by Galileo Galilei. He found that the time it takes for a pendulum to swing is always the same, no matter what the width of the swing is.

LATITUDE The distance in degrees between the parallels.

LEAP-YEAR The year when February has 29 days instead of 28. There is a leap-year every four years.

LOG The instrument for measuring a ship's speed.

LONGITUDE The distance in degrees between the meridians.

LUNAR Relating to the moon.

LUNAR CALENDAR A calendar based on the lunar cycle (month). The Muslim calendar is the only modern lunar calendar.

LUNAR MONTH An interval lasting 29 days, 12 hours, and 44 minutes, which is the time it takes for the moon to go around the earth (see **moon**).

LUNAR PHASES See **phases of the moon**.

LUNAR-SOLAR CALENDAR A calendar which counts the months, basing them on the phases of the moon, yet which works out the year according to the movement of the earth around the sun. The Hebrew and Chinese calendars are lunar-solar.

LUNATION See **lunar month.**

MECHANICAL CLOCK A clock which uses some type of mechanism to show the time.

MERIDIAN An imaginary circle passing through the earth's poles:

MONTH One of the 12 periods into which the year is divided (see **moon**).

MOON A satellite of the earth. It takes about 29 days to go round the earth, (a month). Seen from the earth during this period, it changes in appearance. These changes are the phases of the moon.

MOSQUE A place where Muslims go to pray.

PARALLELS Imaginary circles on the earth's surface, parallel to the equator and perpendicular to the earth's poles.

PENDULUM A weight attached to a freely swinging rope or wire.

PENDULUM CLOCK A mechanical clock. Its movements are made by the swinging of a pendulum.

PHASES OF THE MOON The moon's different aspects seen from the earth: new moon (invisible), first quarter (half moon), full moon (round) and last quarter (half moon).

PHOTOFINISH A television camera which films the finish of the first athletes in speed competitions.

POLAR STAR The star by which sailors used to navigate their ships by.

QUARTZ CLOCK A clock measuring time based on the vibration of a quartz crystal under an electric field.

SEASONS The four divisions of the solar year: spring, summer, autumn and winter.

SEXTANT An instrument which uses the height of the stars to help show the geographical position of a ship.

SOLAR CALENDAR A calendar based on the sun's movement. The months are simple mathematical divisions of the solar year. Our calendar (the Gregorian calendar) is solar.

SOLAR CLOCK See **sundial**.

SOLAR YEAR See **solar calendar**.

SOLSTICES The summer solstice is the longest day in the northern hemisphere; the winter solstice is the shortest day.

SUNDIAL A solar clock made up of a vertical rod (see **gnomon**), whose shadow is projected onto a dial with various markings. The rod's shadow falls onto different parts of the dial according to the time of the day.

TELESCOPE This allows people to observe the stars in the sky, even some which are invisible to the naked eye.

TIME ZONE The earth is divided into 24 meridian time zones. There is one hour's difference between each successive zone. Zero meridian is the one passing through Greenwich, London.

WATER CLOCK The first form of water clock was the clepsydra. Later, the Greeks made many more elaborate water clocks, such as the Tower of the Winds.

YEAR In the Gregorian calendar, this is the period of 12 months from the first of January onwards (see **earth**).

ZIGGURAT Very old Babylonian temples in the shape of a pyramid.

INDEX

Page numbers in **bold** refer to illustrations.